BART SIMPSON
CLASS CLOWN

Drew McWilliam

TITAN BOOKS

BART SIMPSON: CLASS CLOWN

Collects Bart Simpson Comics 33, 34, 35, 36, 37

Copyright © 2006, 2007 and 2010 by
Bongo Entertainment, Inc. All rights reserved.

Published in the UK by Titan Books, a division of Titan Publishing Group,
144 Southwark St., London, SE1 0UP, under licence from Bongo Entertainment, Inc.

FIRST EDITION: MAY 2010

ISBN 9781848567504

2 4 6 8 10 9 7 5 3

Publisher: Matt Groening
Creative Director: Bill Morrison
Managing Editor: Terry Delegeane
Director of Operations: Robert Zaugh
Art Director: Nathan Kane
Art Director Special Projects: Serban Cristescu
Production Manager: Christopher Ungar
Assistant Art Director: Chia-Hsien Jason Ho
Production/Design: Karen Bates, Nathan Hamill, Art Villanueva
Staff Artist: Mike Rote
Administration: Ruth Waytz, Pete Benson
Legal Guardian: Susan A. Grode

Trade Paperback Concepts and Design: Serban Cristescu

Cover: Kevin Newman and Serban Cristescu

Contributing Artists:
Marcos Asprec, Karen Bates, John Costanza, Serban Cristescu, Mike DeCarlo,
Frances Dinglasan, Nathan Hamill , Jason Ho, Nathan Kane, Earl Kress, James Lloyd, Bill Morrison,
Kevin Newman, Joey Nilges, Phyllis Novin, Phil Ortiz, Andrew Pepoy, Mike Rote, Howard Shum,
Steve Steere Jr., Chris Ungar, Carlos Valenti, Art Villanueva

Contributing Writers:
James W. Bates, Tony DiGerolamo, Chuck Dixon, Clay & Susan Griffith,
Tom Peyer, Ty Templeton, Mary Trainor

Printed in Spain

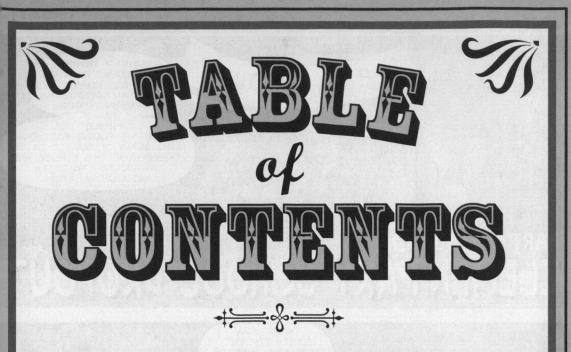

TABLE *of* CONTENTS

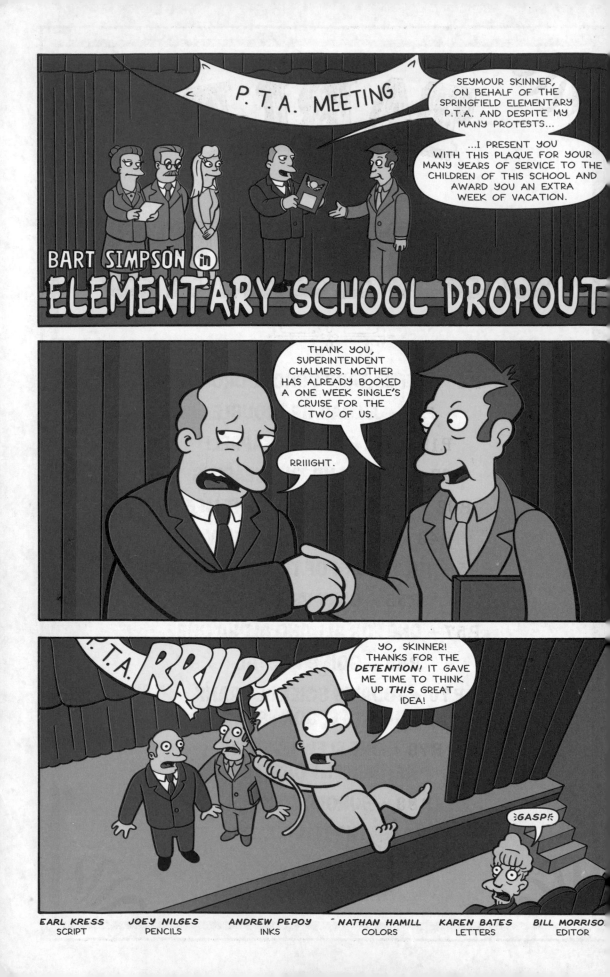

EARL KRESS   JOEY NILGES   ANDREW PEPOY   NATHAN HAMILL   KAREN BATES   BILL MORRISO
SCRIPT   PENCILS   INKS   COLORS   LETTERS   EDITOR

5

7

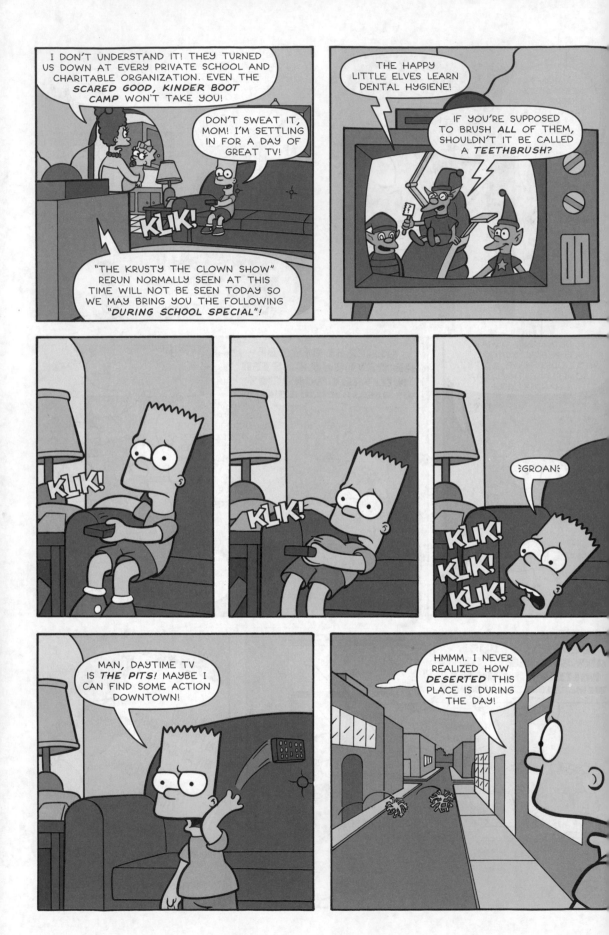

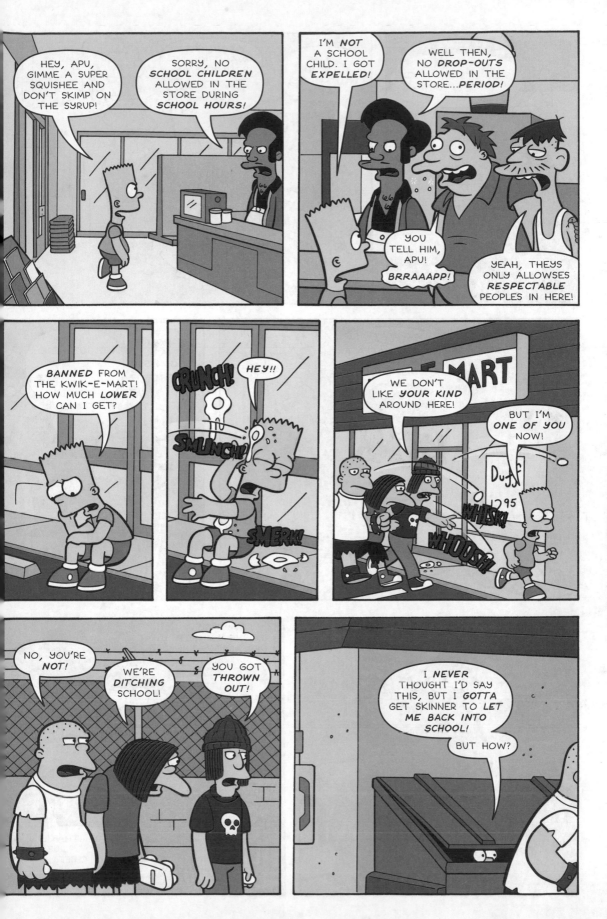

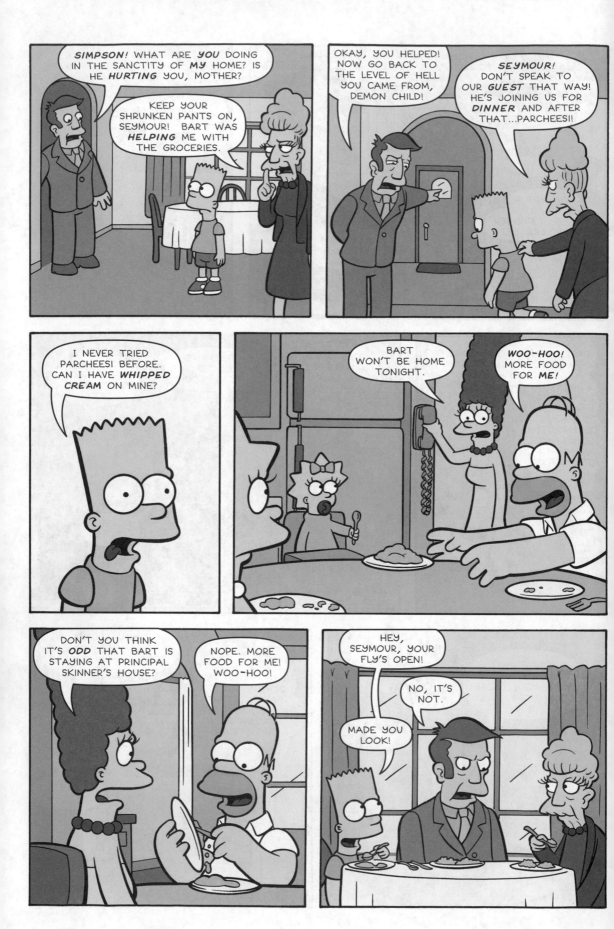

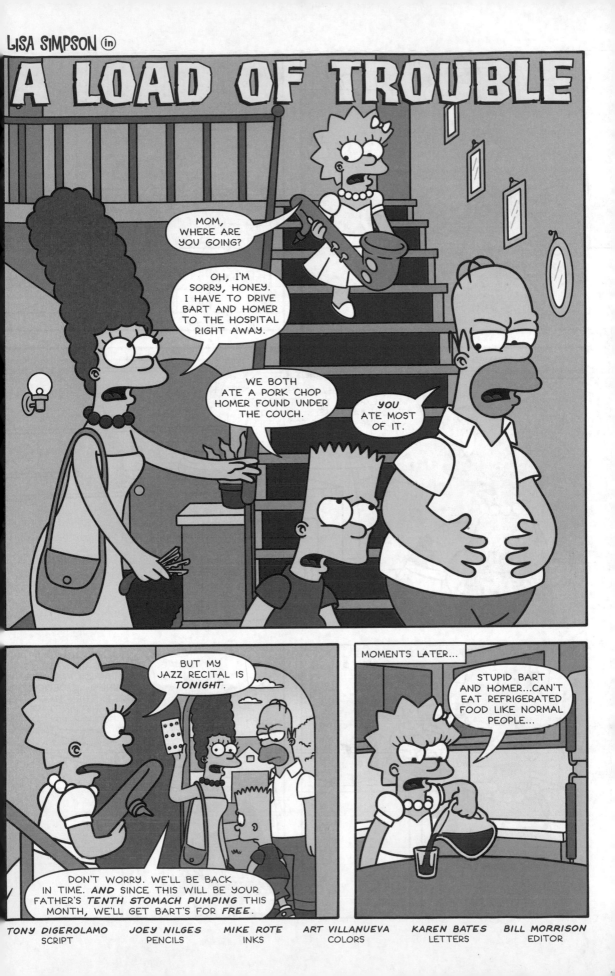

LISA SIMPSON (in)

A LOAD OF TROUBLE

MOM, WHERE ARE YOU GOING?

OH, I'M SORRY, HONEY. I HAVE TO DRIVE BART AND HOMER TO THE HOSPITAL RIGHT AWAY.

WE BOTH ATE A PORK CHOP HOMER FOUND UNDER THE COUCH.

YOU ATE MOST OF IT.

BUT MY JAZZ RECITAL IS *TONIGHT*.

DON'T WORRY. WE'LL BE BACK IN TIME. *AND* SINCE THIS WILL BE YOUR FATHER'S *TENTH STOMACH PUMPING* THIS MONTH, WE'LL GET BART'S FOR *FREE*.

MOMENTS LATER...

STUPID BART AND HOMER...CAN'T EAT REFRIGERATED FOOD LIKE NORMAL PEOPLE...

TONY DIGEROLAMO
SCRIPT

JOEY NILGES
PENCILS

MIKE ROTE
INKS

ART VILLANUEVA
COLORS

KAREN BATES
LETTERS

BILL MORRISON
EDITOR

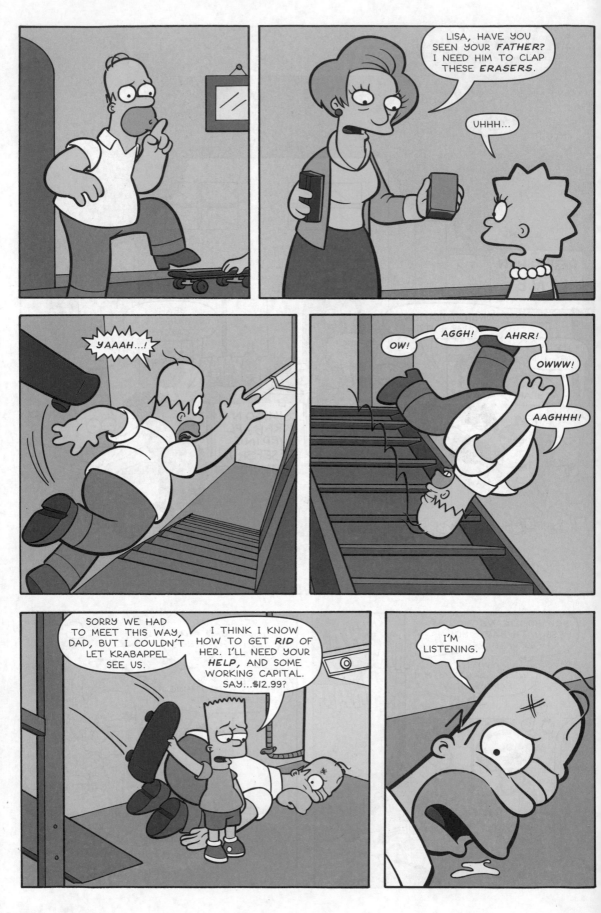

"WE RELEASED OUR FIRST RECORD, *ME LOVE'S IN THE LOO,* AND IT WENT STRAIGHT TO NUMBER ONE IN SCOTLAND!"

"WE COULD NAE WALK THE STREETS OF GLASGOW, EDINBURGH, OR ABERDEEN WITHOUT BEING MOBBED."

"I WAS NOT THEN THE COARSE GALOOT YOU SEE BEFORE YOU. BACK THEN, I HAD A MOST AGREEABLE COUNTENANCE, AND, I DARE SAY, I WAS A BIT OF A DANDY."

"I WAS THE FIRST TO WEAR A MINI-KILT."

"AND IT WAS *I* WHO INVENTED *THE WEASEL HAIRCUT*...BRUSHING ME EYEBROWS UP AND OVER ME FOREHEAD."

"*OCH!* BUT MY FASHION SENSE AND CHARISMA WAS MY UNDOING. YOU SEE, ALL THE LASSIES WERE MAD FOR ME."

"I AVERAGED OVER 800 MARRIAGE PROPOSALS A DAY!"

Dear Willie,
Marry me and
fly for free!
Fiona McFadden
Stewardess,
Air Scotland

"I'D SHAKE MY HEAD AND GO "WOOOOOO," AND THE BONNIE GIRLS WOULD SCREAM AND THROW HAGGIS UP ON THE STAGE."

WEE LOVE WEE WILLIE!

WILLIE! WON'T HE?

THE OTHER WEASELS COULDN'T STAND IT. JEALOUS THEY WERE OF ME GOOD LOOKS AND FIERCE WAY WITH A SNARE DRUM."

"AND SO, WHILST ON OUR FIRST TRIP TO AMERICA, THEY DITCHED ME HERE IN SPRINGFIELD AND REPLACED ME WITH SOME LIVERPUDLIAN IDIOT. "BLINGO" THEY CALLED HIM, BECAUSE OF ALL THE JEWELRY HE WORE."

ONE BEAUTIFUL SATURDAY MORNING IN SPRINGFIELD...

BART SIMPSON in
SIGNS OF INTELLIGENT LIFE

I'M BORED!

WHY DID MILHOUSE HAVE TO GO TO THAT STUPID *ALLERGY* CAMP?

CLAY & SUSAN GRIFFITH
SCRIPT

PHIL ORTIZ
PENCILS

MIKE DECARLO
INKS

NATHAN HAMILL
COLORS

KAREN BATES
LETTERS

BILL MORRISON
EDITOR

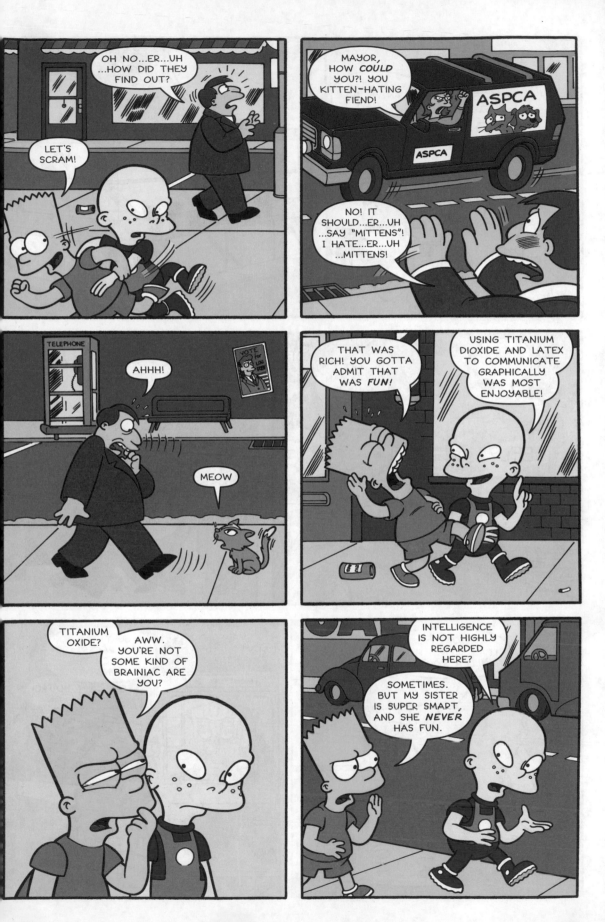

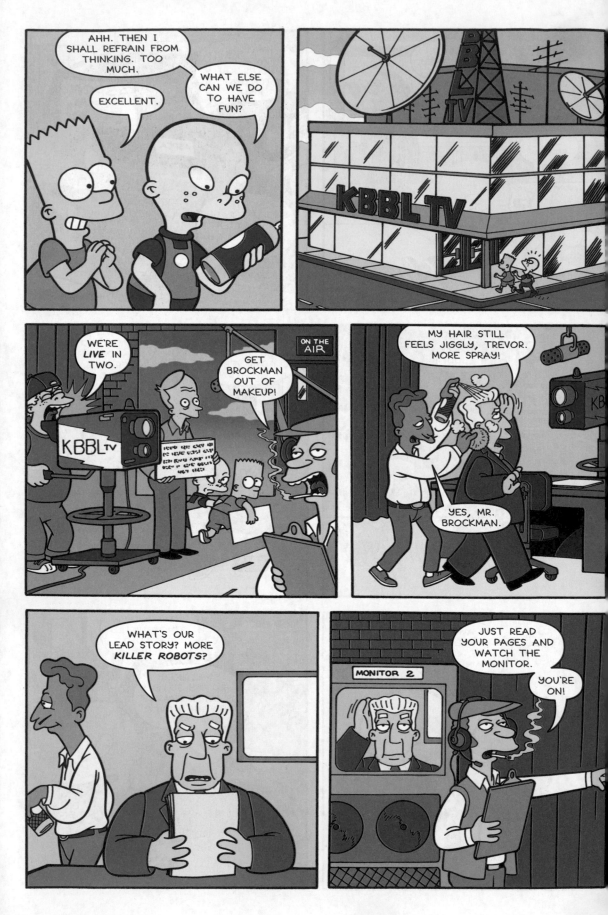

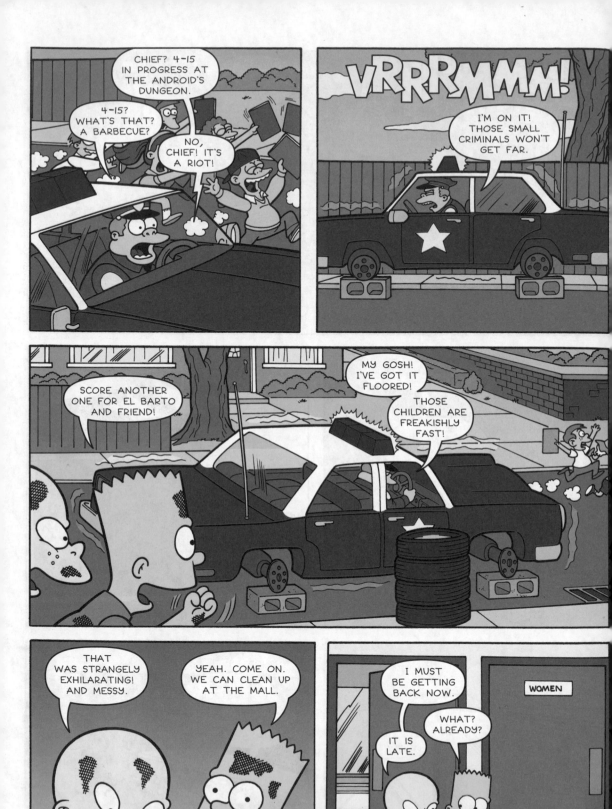

TOM PEYER
SCRIPT

MARCOS APSREC
PENCILS

MIKE ROTE
INKS

ART VILLANUEVA
COLORS

KAREN BATES
LETTERS

BILL MORRISON
EDITOR

MATT GROENING presents

BART SIMPSON in
THE RETURN OF TRUCKASAURUS

JAMES BATES
SCRIPT

CARLOS VALENTI
PENCILS

STEVE STEERE, JR.
INKS

NATHAN HAMILL
COLORS

KAREN BATES
LETTERS

BILL MORRISON
EDITOR

WHAT GIVES?

HEY, BART! I'M HAVIN' A LITTLE ENGINE TROUBLE.

¡HACK! COUGH!¡ I CAN SEE THAT! HOW CAN YOU BREATHE?

NO PROBLEMO. SMOKE DOESN'T BOTHER ME.

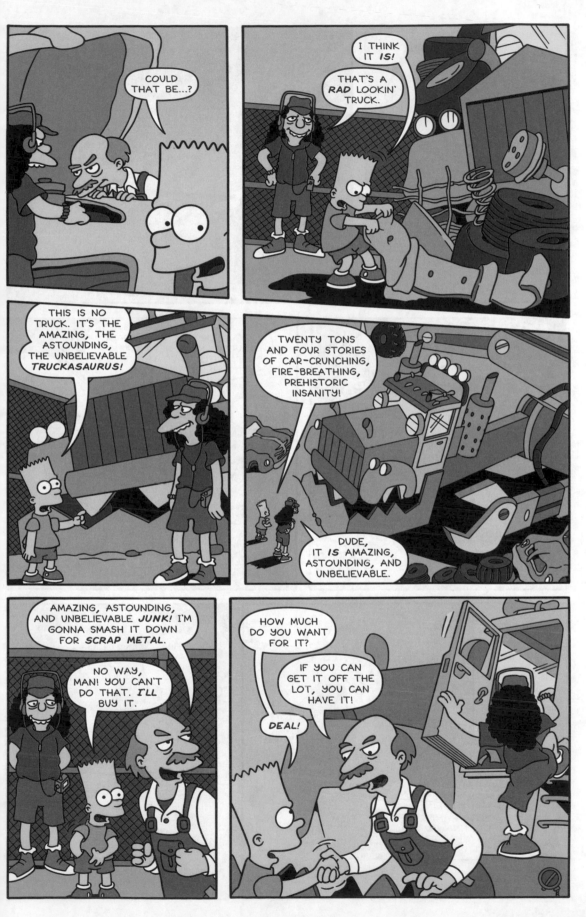

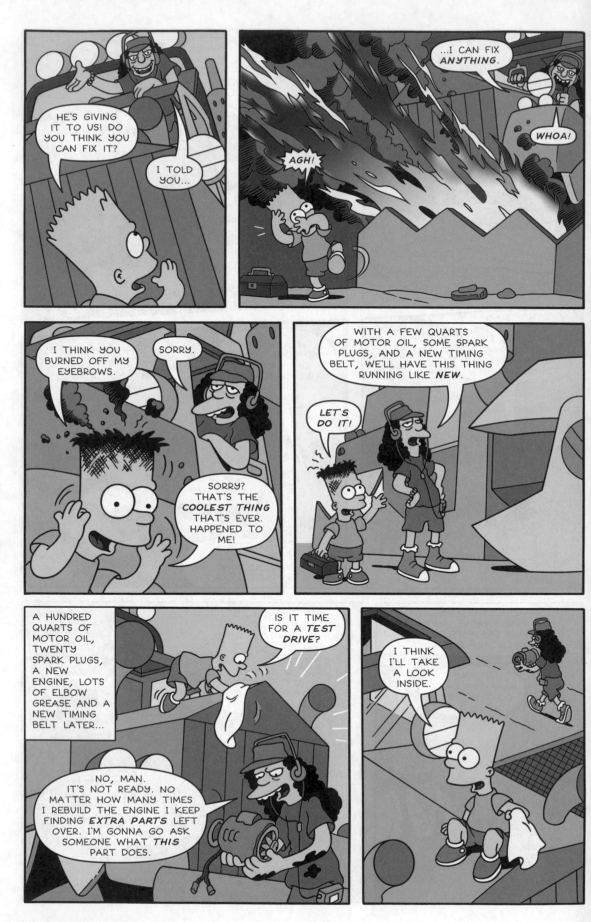

49

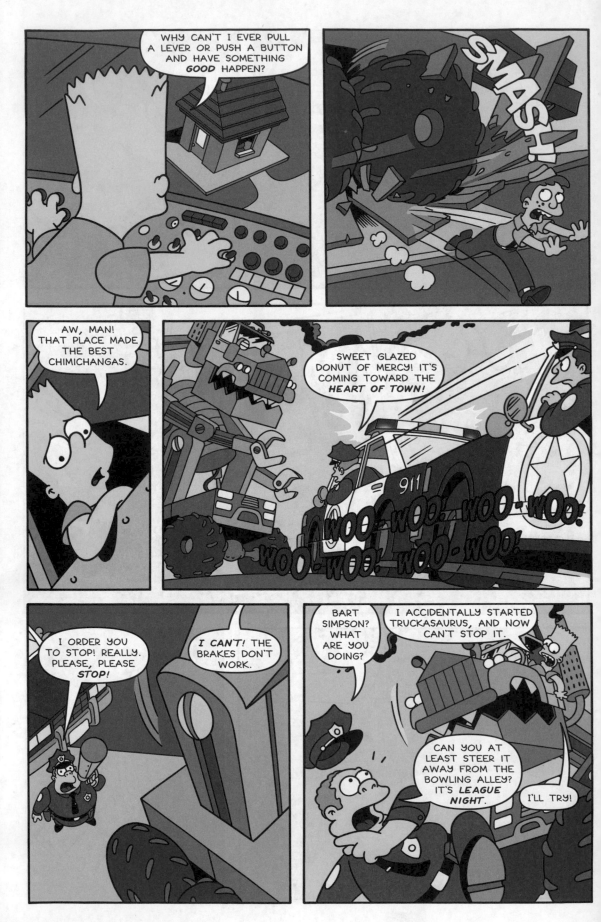

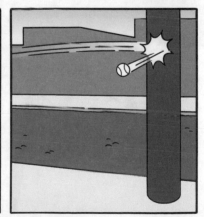

MARY TRAINOR
CRIPT & LAYOUTS

JASON HO
PENCILS

MIKE ROTE
INKS

ART VILLANUEVA
COLORS

KAREN BATES
LETTERS

BILL MORRISON
EDITOR

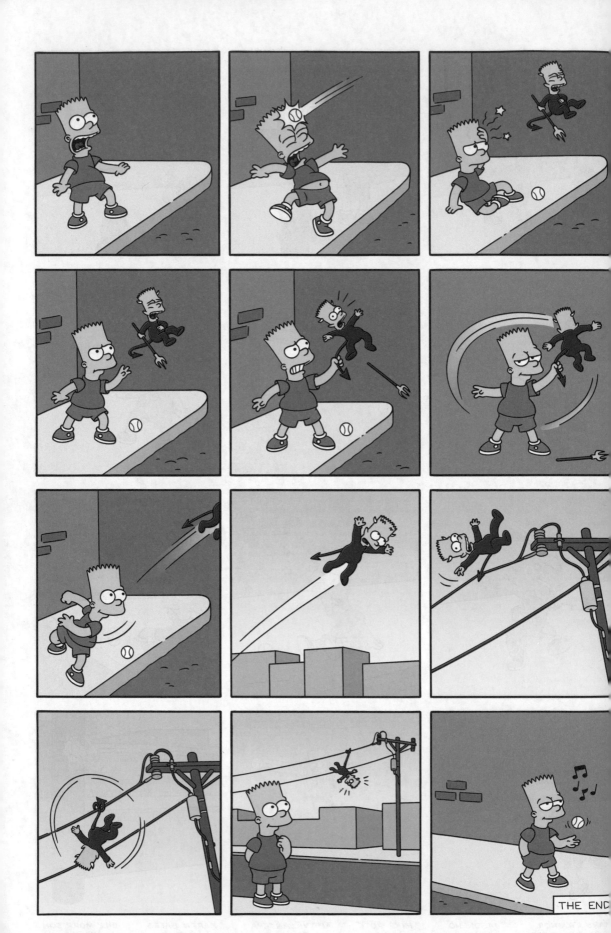

THE END

ARY TRAINOR
SCRIPT

JAMES LLOYD
PENCILS

ANDREW PEPOY
INKS

NATHAN HAMILL
COLORS

KAREN BATES
LETTERS

BILL MORRISON
EDITOR

58

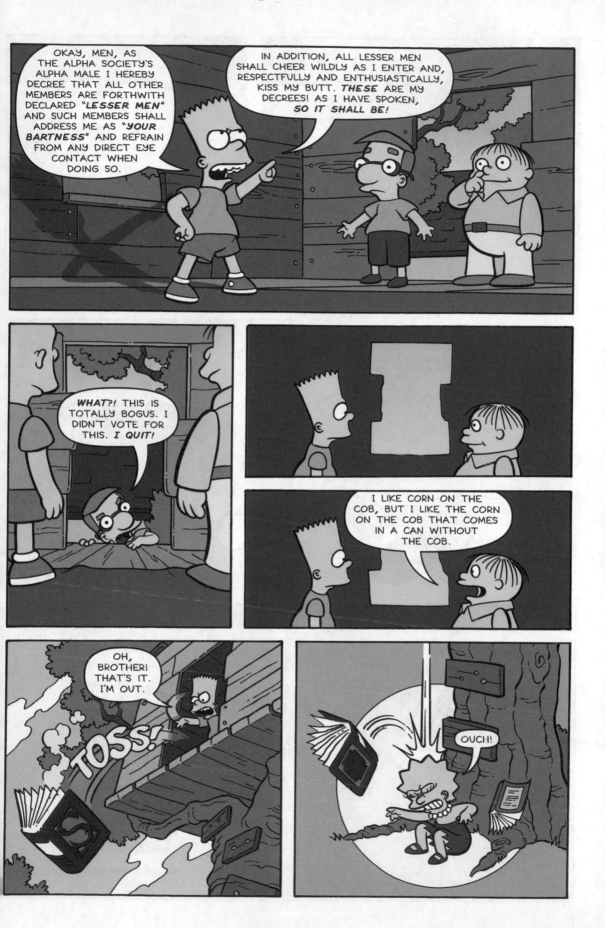

ARY TRAINOR
SCRIPT

JASON HO
PENCILS

MIKE ROTE
INKS

CHRIS UNGAR
COLORS

KAREN BATES
LETTERS

BILL MORRISON
EDITOR

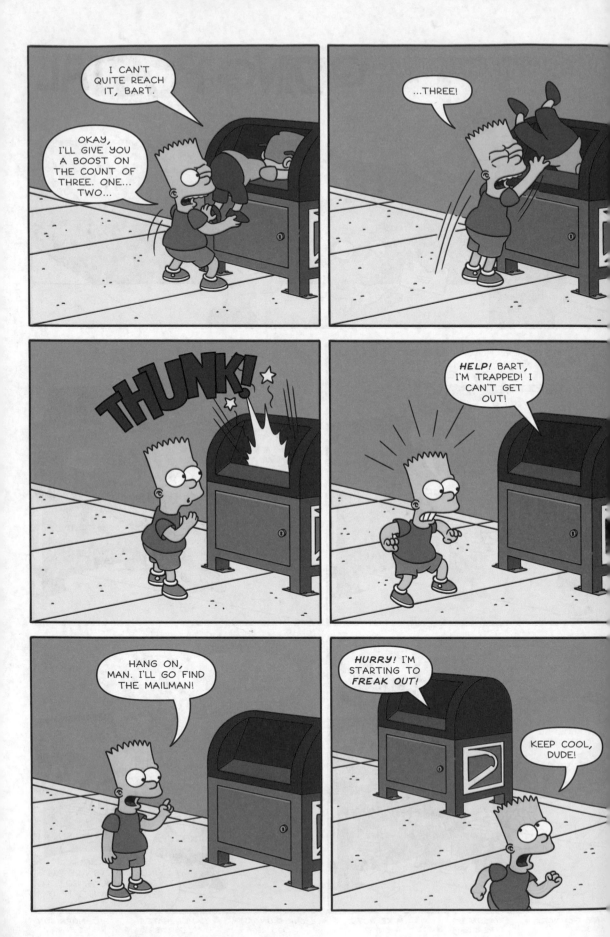

TONY DIGEROLAMO
SCRIPT

FRANCES DINGLASAN
PENCILS

HOWARD SHUM
INKS

ART VILLANUEVA
COLORS

KAREN BATES
LETTERS

BILL MORRISON
EDITOR

BART SIMPSON IN

ONE FLEW OVER THE RETIREMENT CASTLE

SPRINGFIELD RETIREMENT CASTLE

SCREEEECH!

GO ON, BOY. YOUR REPORT'S NOT GOING TO WRITE ITSELF.

CAN'T I JUST COPY STUFF OUT OF AN ENCYCLOPEDIA AND RENT A COSTUME?

IT'S NOT JUST GRAMPA. IT'S ALL THOSE OLD PEOPLE. THEY'RE DEPRESSING!

THAT'S WHY THEY'RE THE PERFECT ONES TO TALK TO ABOUT *THE GREAT DEPRESSION*!

YOU'LL BE BACK SOON, RIGHT?

SHAME ON YOU, BOY. OLD PEOPLE DESERVE YOUR RESPECT...NOW GET IN THERE SO I CAN GET AWAY BEFORE THE OLD MAN SEES ME AND I HAVE TO GO IN, TOO!

JAMES W. BATES
SCRIPT

JOEY NILGES
PENCILS

MIKE ROTE
INKS

NATHAN HAMILL
COLORS

KAREN BATES
LETTERS

BILL MORRISON
EDITOR

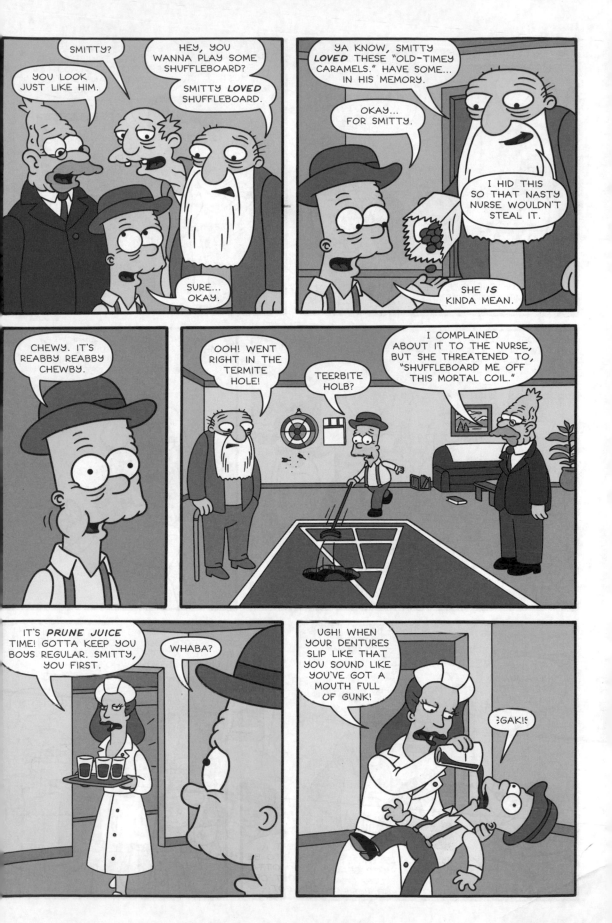

79

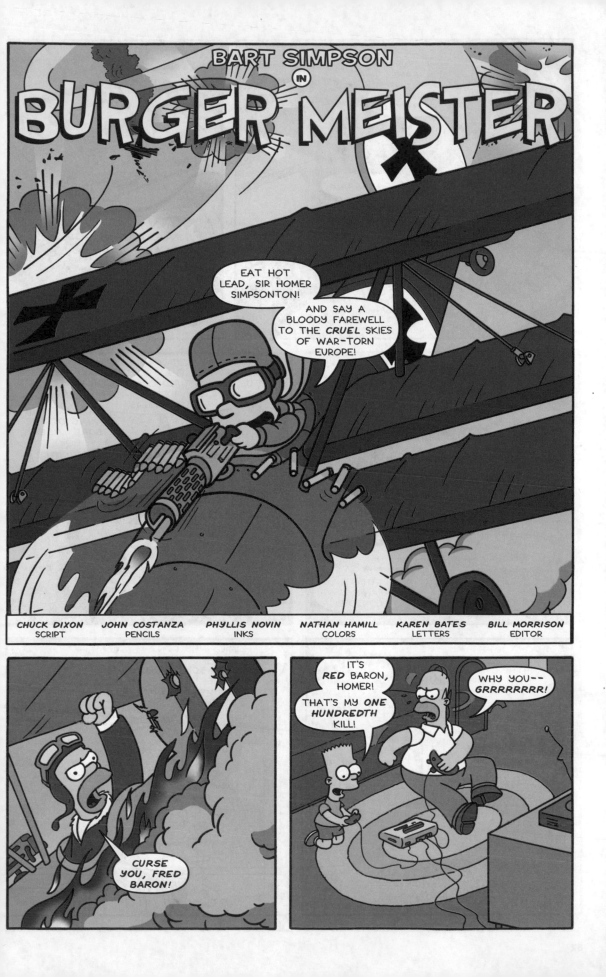

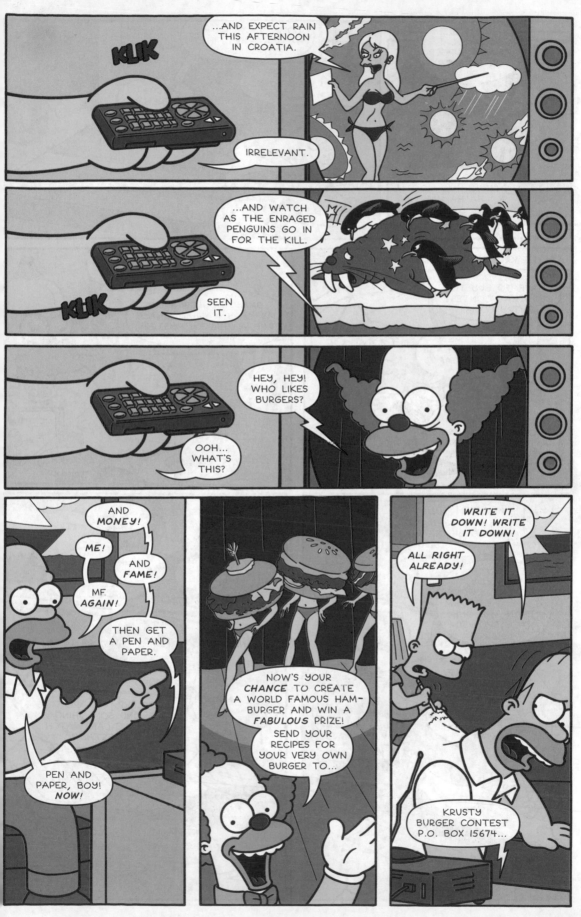

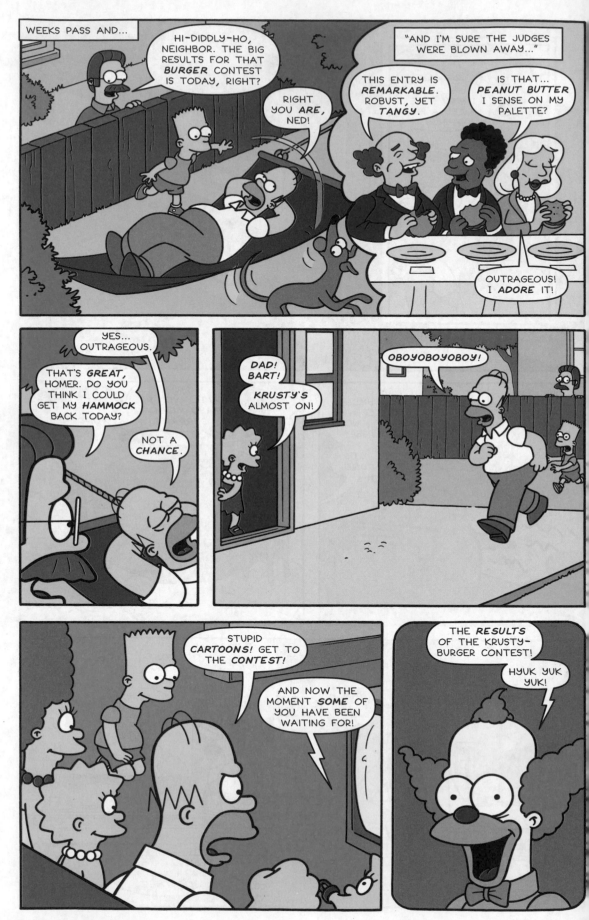

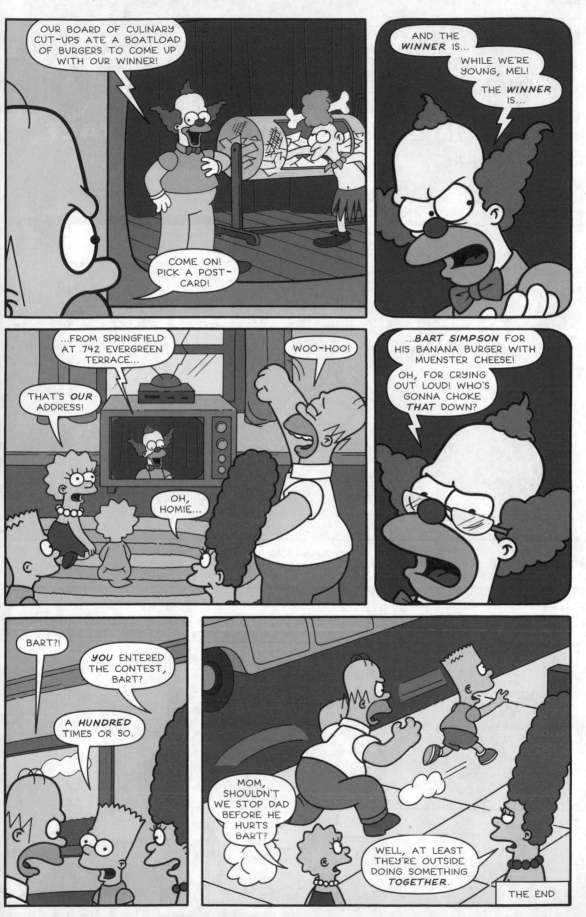

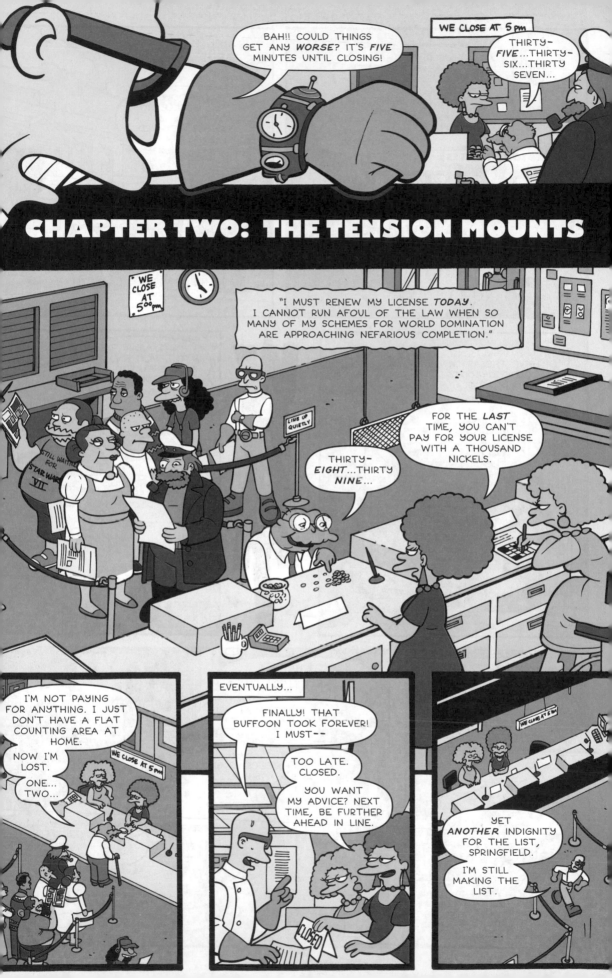

CHAPTER TWO: THE TENSION MOUNTS

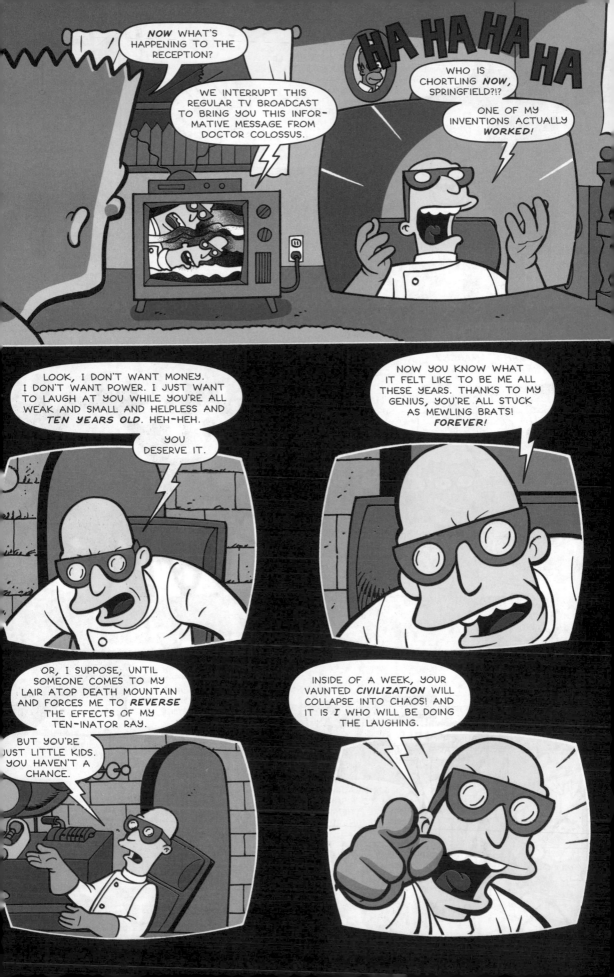

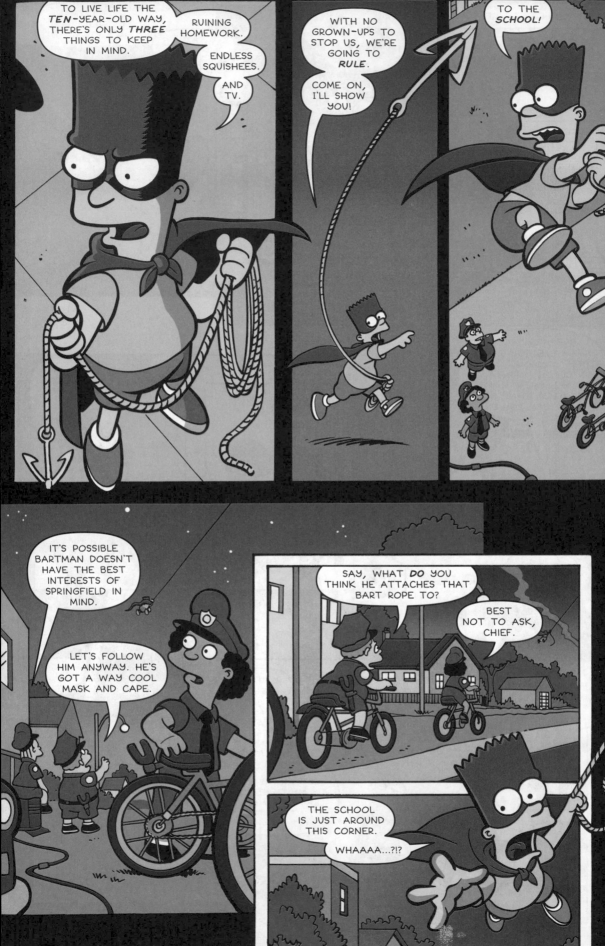

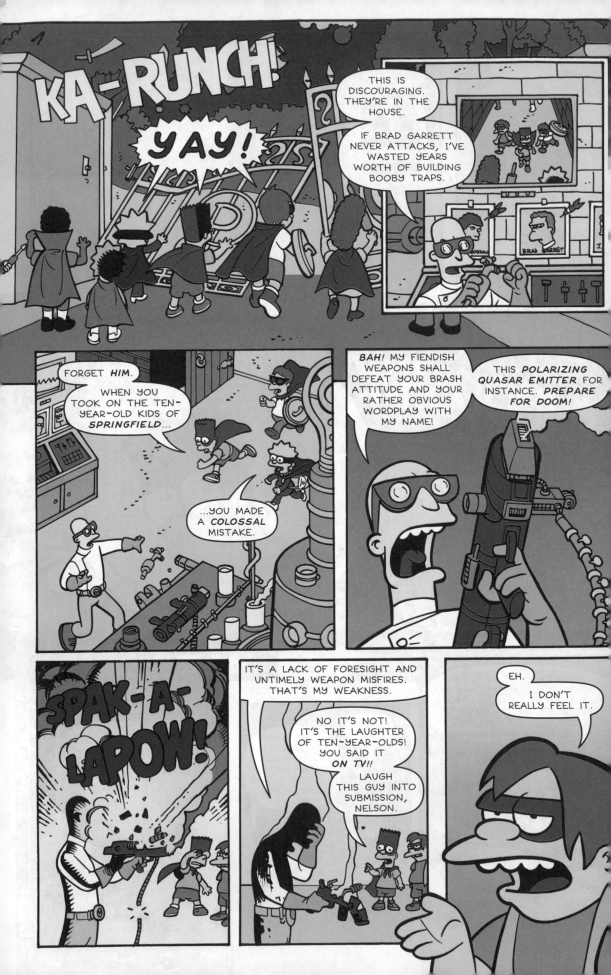

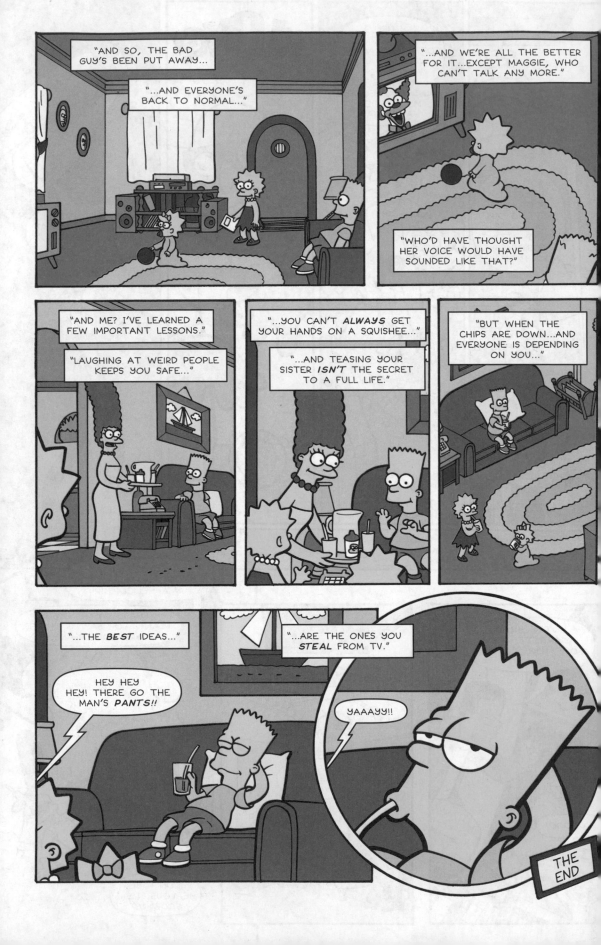